T0045865

PRESENTED TO:

_____

FROM:

_____

DATE:

_____

THE ENNEAGRAM COLLECTION
THE PROTECTIVE CHALLENGER

ENNEAGRAM TYPE 8

BETH McCORD

Your **Enneagram** Coach

THOMAS NELSON
Since 1798

Enneagram Type 8: The Protective Challenger

Published in Nashville, Tennessee, by Thomas Nelson. Thomas Nelson is a registered trademark of HarperCollins Christian Publishing, Inc.

Published in association with Alive Literary Agency.

Graphic Designer: Jane Butler, Well Refined Creative Director, wellrefined.co
Interior Designer: Emily Ghattas
Cover Designer: Greg Jackson at Thinkpen Design

ISBN-13: 978-1-4002-1574-4

Printed in China

22 23 24 25 26 GRI 11 10 9 8 7 6 5 4

Contents

Foreword

Steamroller, bulldozer, intense and *intimidating* are just a few of the words that have been used to describe me throughout my life. But the funny thing is, I never understood why. What I know *now* is that I am an Enneagram 8.

From an emotional wound I received when I was eight years old, I learned very quickly that I couldn't trust anyone. I learned to cope in my world by controlling my environment and avoiding helplessness at all costs. My motto in high school and college was: carry cash, always drive, and don't trust anyone.

The truth is, I was hard. Very hard.

And as you can imagine, this life strategy came with a wide range of problems. That's why I'm so glad I heard about the Enneagram a few years ago. As I've learned about my personality style, I've been able to know where to grow. I can understand why I do what I do, and I can understand others at a deeper level as well. Yes, I am a classic, textbook Enneagram 8 with a 7 wing, and although 8's tend to have a reputation for being terrifying, I'm actually really proud to be an 8. I'm proud to be someone who stands up for others, speaks up, and gets things done.

But as with any personality style, I also have some major flaws—flaws that not only harm my relationships, but also keep me from the one true calling I have on this earth: to become more like Jesus.

For example, just a couple of years ago, God took me through a wilderness season where I was being wronged at every turn. Week after week and month after month, I was being taken advantage of, falsely accused, and humiliated. Everything in me was screaming at the injustice of it all.

Finally, one day I cried out to God and said, "God, *what* are you doing? Do you even see what's happening?"

Immediately, I felt the most gentle whisper in my spirit respond and say, *Christy, I know that you can stand up and speak up, but can you sit down and take it? I know that you can fight, but can you turn the other cheek?*

The truth is, I couldn't. There were some virtues of being a Christ-follower that came very naturally to me, but there were many that didn't—and still don't, to be honest. Things like patience, gentleness, forgiveness, and trust to name just a few. As you can imagine, God has done some work in me. He began really softening my heart in college and through different seasons and life stages, and He has continued to peel away layers of pride and anger that I didn't even realize I had.

That's why I'm so thankful for Beth McCord's writing. While the Enneagram has helped me understand *where* to grow, Beth McCord has helped me understand *how* to grow. And much more than that, she's taken the tool of the Enneagram and applied it through the lens of Scripture. Everything you'll read in this book will not only help you understand yourself so that you can become who you were created to be, it will also help you grow a deeper relationship with your Creator.

This work won't necessarily be easy, but growth and transformation rarely are. But I promise you this: if you're willing to do the work, it will have an impact on your life, your relationships, and believe it or not, a ripple effect to our entire world in ways you don't even realize right now.

I'm so proud of you for taking this brave step, and I can't wait to see what God is going to do in you—and through you—because of it.

"Let your light shine . . ."
MATTHEW 5:16

Christy Wright, #1 National Bestselling Author, Inspiring Speaker, and Certified Business Coach

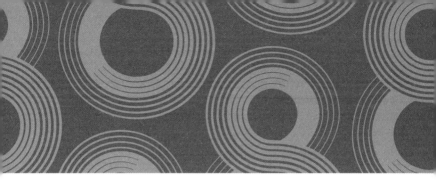

Introduction

I'm so glad you're here! As an Enneagram teacher and coach, I have seen so many lives changed by the Enneagram. This is a perfect place for you to start your own journey of growth. I'll explain how this interactive book works, but first I'd like to share a little of my story.

Before I learned about the Enneagram, I often unknowingly committed *assumicide*, which is my word for damaging a relationship by assuming I know someone's thoughts, feelings, and motivations. I incorrectly guess why someone is behaving a particular way and respond (sometimes with disastrous results) without asking clarifying questions to confirm my assumptions or to find out what actually is going on. I've made many wrong and hurtful assumptions about people I dearly love, as well as destructive presumptions about myself.

When my husband, Jeff, and I were in the early years of our marriage, it was a difficult season in our relationship. For the life of me, I couldn't figure out Jeff, or myself. I had been a Christian since I was young and desired to live like Christ, but I kept running into the same stumbling blocks over and over again. I was constantly frustrated, and I longed to understand my heart's motives—*Why do I do what I do?* I figured understanding that might help jolt me out of my rut, but I didn't know where to start.

Then I learned about the insightful tool of the Enneagram, and it was exactly what I needed.

This personality typology (*ennea* for nine; *gram* for diagram) goes beyond what we do (our behaviors) and gets at *why* we do what we do (our heart's motives). And though there are just nine basic personality Types, each Type has multiple layers, allowing for numerous variations of any given personality Type.

The purpose of the Enneagram is to awaken self-awareness and provide hope for growth. Once we learn why each Type thinks, feels, and acts in specific ways, we can look at ourselves with new understanding. Then we can depend on God in new ways to reshape us. The Enneagram makes us aware of when our heart's motives are good and we are on the best path for our personality Type and when our heart is struggling and veering off course. **The Enneagram is an insightful tool, but God's truth is what sets us free and brings transformation.**

When I first learned about the Enneagram, I resonated with the Type 9—and had a good laugh when I discovered that 9s know themselves the least! But I finally had wisdom that cleared away the fog and illuminated my inner world. I kept thinking, *Oh, that's why I do that!* Everything started making sense, which brought my restless heart relief.

The Enneagram also helped me see when my heart was aligned with God's truth, misaligned to some degree, or out of alignment entirely with the person God created me to be. It would highlight where I was misunderstanding myself or those I love, and then I could use that awareness to seek transformation. Using the Enneagram from this perspective was a significant turning point for me in all my relationships, especially my marriage. My new perspective allowed me to have more compassion, kindness, forgiveness, mercy, and grace toward others and myself.

Exploring my heart has been some of the hardest—and most rewarding—work I've ever done. The process of looking at our hearts exposes who we are at the core, which highlights our need for redemption and care from God, who is always supplying us with what we need. We simply need to come to Him and depend on Him to change us from the inside out. He will give us a new internal peace, joy, and security that will help us to flourish in new and life-giving ways.

The Enneagram can function as an internal GPS, helping you understand why you and others think, feel, and behave in particular ways.

This internal GPS assists you in knowing your current location (your Main Enneagram Type) and your Type's healthiest destination (how your Type can live in alignment with the gospel).

The Enneagram also acts like a rumble strip on the highway—that boundary that makes an irritating sound when your car touches it, warning you when you're about to go off course. It keeps you from swerving into dangerous situations.

While everyone has character traits of all nine Types to varying degrees, we call only one our Main Type. In this book you will unlock some of the mysteries behind *why* you do what you do and discern ways you can grow into your best self.

If you're not sure of your Type number, that's okay! Going through the exercises will help you figure out what your Type number is. Sometimes it's helpful to find out what we're *not* as much as what we are. It's all about self-discovery and self-awareness.

If you find you resonate more with another number, that insight is valuable.

• • •

In the twenty-one entries that follow, we'll begin with a summary of your Type. Then we'll discuss topics that are general to the Enneagram and specific to your Type. Each reading will end with reflection questions—prompts to help you write out your thoughts, feelings, and gut reactions to what you have read. Putting pen to paper will help you focus and process what is going on inside you.

Before you begin, I want you to commit to observing your inner world from a nonjudgmental stance. Since God has fully forgiven us, we can observe ourselves without condemnation, guilt, or shame. Instead, we can rest in the fact that we are unconditionally loved, forgiven, and accepted based on what Christ did for us. Follow the prompts and write about your own story. Allow God to transform you from the inside out by helping you see yourself through the lens of the beautiful and amazing Type He designed you to be.

It's my privilege to walk with you as you discover who you are by examining your heart. I'm excited to be on this journey with you!

TYPE 8
I'M THANKFUL FOR YOU BECAUSE...

You are an excellent natural leader who others look up to. You have no problem taking the initiative to make things happen. You are a champion of people, a provider, a protector, honorable, and support others with your strength. Those close to you know they are safe and protected.

OVERVIEW OF THE NINE ENNEAGRAM TYPES

The Enneagram (*ennea* = nine, *gram* = diagram) is a map for personal growth that identifies the nine basic ways of relating to and perceiving the world. It accurately describes *why* you think, feel, and behave in particular ways based upon your Core Motivations. Understanding the Enneagram will give you more self-awareness, forgiveness, and compassion for yourself and others.

To find your main Type, take our FREE assessment at test.YourEnneagramCoach.com, and find the Type on the next page that has your Core Motivations—what activates and drives your thoughts, feelings, and behaviors.

Core Motivations of Each Type

 Core Desires: what you're always striving for, believing it will completely fulfill you

 Core Fears: what you're always avoiding and trying to prevent from happening

 Core Weakness: the issue you're always wrestling with, which will remain a struggle until you're in heaven and is a reminder you need God's help on a daily basis

 Core Longing: the message your heart is always longing to hear

Type 1: MORAL PERFECTIONIST

 Core Desire: Having integrity; being good, balanced, accurate, virtuous, and right.

 Core Fear: Being wrong, bad, evil, inappropriate, unredeemable, or corruptible.

 Core Weakness: *Resentment*: Repressing anger that leads to continual frustration and dissatisfaction with yourself, others, and the world for not being perfect.

 Core Longing: You are good.

Type 2: SUPPORTIVE ADVISOR

Core Desire: Being appreciated, loved, and wanted.

Core Fear: Being rejected and unwanted; being thought worthless, needy, inconsequential, dispensable, or unworthy of love.

Core Weakness: *Pride*: Denying your own needs and emotions while using your strong intuition to discover and focus on the emotions and needs of others; confidently inserting your helpful support in hopes that others will say how grateful they are for your thoughtful care.

Core Longing: You are wanted and loved.

Type 3: SUCCESSFUL ACHIEVER

Core Desire: Having high status and respect; being admired, successful, and valuable.

Core Fear: Being exposed as or thought incompetent, inefficient, or worthless; failing to be or appear successful.

Core Weakness: *Deceit*: Deceiving yourself into believing that you are only the image you present to others; embellishing the truth by putting on a polished persona for everyone (including yourself) to see and admire.

Core Longing: You are loved for simply being you.

Type 4: ROMANTIC INDIVIDUALIST

Core Desire: Being unique, special, and authentic.

Core Fear: Being inadequate, emotionally cut off, plain, mundane, defective, flawed, or insignificant.

Core Weakness: *Envy*: Feeling that you're tragically flawed, that something foundational is missing inside you, and that others possess qualities you lack.

Core Longing: You are seen and loved for exactly who you are—special and unique.

Type 5: INVESTIGATIVE THINKER

Core Desire: Being capable and competent.

Core Fear: Being annihilated, invaded, or not existing; being thought incapable or ignorant; having obligations placed upon you, or your energy being completely depleted.

Core Weakness: *Avarice*: Feeling that you lack inner resources and that too much interaction with others will lead to catastrophic depletion; withholding yourself from contact with the world; holding on to your resources and minimizing your needs.

Core Longing: Your needs are not a problem.

Type 6: LOYAL GUARDIAN

☀ **Core Desire:** Having security, guidance, and support.

🛡 **Core Fear:** Fearing fear itself; being without support, security, or guidance; being blamed, targeted, alone, or physically abandoned.

 Core Weakness: *Anxiety*: Scanning the horizon of life and trying to predict and prevent negative outcomes (especially worst-case scenarios); remaining in a constant state of apprehension and worry.

🔥 **Core Longing:** You are safe and secure.

Type 7: ENTERTAINING OPTIMIST

☀ **Core Desire:** Being happy, fully satisfied, and content.

🛡 **Core Fear:** Being deprived, trapped in emotional pain, limited, or bored; missing out on something fun.

 Core Weakness: *Gluttony*: Feeling a great emptiness inside and having an insatiable desire to "fill yourself up" with experiences and stimulation in hopes of feeling completely satisfied and content.

🔥 **Core Longing:** You will be taken care of.

Type 8: PROTECTIVE CHALLENGER

☀ **Core Desire:** Protecting yourself and those in your inner circle.

❗ **Core Fear:** Being weak, powerless, harmed, controlled, vulnerable, manipulated, and left at the mercy of injustice.

❄ **Core Weakness:** *Lust/Excess:* Constantly desiring intensity, control, and power; willfully pushing yourself on others in order to get what you desire.

🔥 **Core Longing:** You will not be betrayed.

Type 9: PEACEFUL MEDIATOR

☀ **Core Desire:** Having inner stability and peace of mind.

❗ **Core Fear:** Being in conflict, tension, or discord; feeling shut out and overlooked; losing connection and relationship with others.

❄ **Core Weakness:** *Sloth:* Remaining in an unrealistic and idealistic world in order to keep the peace, remain easygoing, and not be disturbed by your anger; falling asleep to your passions, abilities, desires, needs, and worth by merging with others to keep peace and harmony.

🔥 **Core Longing:** Your presence matters.

TYPE 8
KEY MOTIVATIONS

Eights are motivated to protect themselves and those who are left at the mercy of injustice. They want to be strong, autonomous, direct, in control, and invincible as they assert themselves throughout all of life.

Overview of Type 8

The Protective Challenger

**Assertive | Self-Confident | Intense
Bighearted | Confrontational**

You walk through life with confident intensity, strength, and a determination to make things happen. Your decisive and assertive leadership style makes you a powerful change agent in the world, especially when seeking justice and protection for others.

However, in our unjust world where people take advantage of each other, you feel you must protect yourself from betrayal and powerlessness. You do so by having an invincible exterior and minimizing personal vulnerability, keeping a thick piece of steel over your extremely tender heart.

While other Types fear people and become passive, you fear people and become aggressive. If you're concerned someone might betray you, you'll think, *I'll control you before you can control me.* Your fear of weakness combined with your thirst for control and justice can lead you to be confrontational, insensitive, domineering, cynical, too blunt, and even vengeful.

You live in denial about any emotions or weaknesses that cause you to be vulnerable or out of control. In relationships with others, you can end up sacrificing intimacy so that weaknesses can't be discovered and used against you. Denying yourself closeness with others through vulnerability, tenderness, and the giving and receiving of forgiveness leaves you incomplete, not experiencing the intimate and supportive relationships you were created for.

But when your heart surrenders your fear of

betrayal and relies on God, you can relinquish your need for control and allow others to see an endearing vulnerability and compassionate strength within you. Then you can better protect the innocent from injustice, empower others, and put your strength of leadership to use for the greater good.

Faith and the Enneagram

Is your heart a mystery to you? Do you need help using the knowledge the Enneagram offers to improve your life? If that's where you are, I'm happy to tell you that there is help and there is hope.

The Bible teaches that God cares about our heart's motives. He "sees not as man sees: man looks on the outward appearance, but the LORD looks on the heart" (1 Samuel 16:7). So we shouldn't look only at our external behaviors; we also need to examine our inner world. For most of us, it's no surprise that the heart of our problem is the problem of our heart!

Before we begin discussing the Enneagram in depth, I'd like to share my beliefs with you for two reasons: First, it's a critical part of how I'll guide you through the Enneagram principles. Second, my faith is what sustains and encourages me, and I believe the same will be true for you.

I believe the Bible is God's truth and the ultimate authority for our lives. Through it, we learn about God's character, love, and wisdom. It brings us close to Him and guides us in the best way to live. My relationship with God brought me healing and purpose before I ever heard of the Enneagram.

Jesus has not been optional for my personal growth; He has been absolutely and utterly vital. He has always come alongside me with love, compassion, and mercy.

I've always wanted my faith to be the most important part of my life, but I spent years frustrated, running into the same issues in my heart over and over again. The Enneagram helped me understand my heart's motives.

As you think about your Type, I'll help you look

at your heart, your life, and your relationships through the lens of the Enneagram. I'll also teach you ways to understand yourself and others and to develop patience and empathy for your differences.

With God working in you and helpful insights from the Enneagram to change awareness and actions, you'll grow into the person you'd like to be more than you've ever dared to dream possible.

When you place your faith in Jesus Christ as your Savior, three life-changing questions are answered, bringing you ultimate grace and freedom:

Am I fully accepted by God (even with all the mess and sin in my life)?

Yes! You are declared righteous. Christ not only purchased forgiveness for your sin but also gave you His perfect righteousness.

Am I loved by God?

Yes! God cherishes you and wants you to be close to Him. He adopted you, making you His beloved child.

Is it really possible for me to change?

Yes! You are being made new. This both *happened* to you and *is happening* to you. This means that you are changed because of what Christ has done, and you are continuing to change as you grow in Christ (it's a bit of a paradox). You can live in an ongoing process of growth by working with the Holy Spirit to become more like Christ, who loves you and gave Himself up for you.

These three life-changing events are what we mean by God's truth, the good news of Christ's finished work on our behalf—"the gospel."

Receiving God's truth and learning about the Enneagram will give you a deeper and richer understanding of *who you are* and *Whose you are*.

When we know *who we are*, we understand our heart's motives and needs and can see God reaching out to meet our needs and giving us grace for our sins through Christ.

And when we know *Whose we are*, we understand that because of Christ's sacrifice on our behalf, we're God's cherished children. He comforts, sustains, and delights in us. Because of God's character, His love never changes; it doesn't depend on us "getting better" or "doing better" since it hinges solely on what Christ has already done for us. He loves us and desires for us to be in a relationship with Him. We become more like Him by surrendering to Him and depending on the Holy Spirit to transform us.

Which leads us back to looking at who we are. Bringing our faith and the Enneagram together helps us hear God's truths in our mother tongue (kind of like our personality Type's unique language), which enables us to understand God's truth more deeply and will lead to transformation.

Going Deeper

What things have you longed to change about yourself?

_____

_____

_____

_____

_____

_____

_____

_____

_____

How have you attempted to rescue yourself in the past or bring about change on your own? How successful were you?

_____

_____

_____

_____

_____

_____

_____

_____

_____

_____

_____

What difference does knowing you belong to God make in your life?

_____

_____

_____

_____

_____

_____

_____

_____

_____

_____

Being Aware

We can't do anything to make God love us more or love us less since our relationship status has been taken care of solely through Christ's finished work on our behalf. And yet that doesn't mean we're not responsible for participating in our growth. That growth path will look different for different personality Types. We can use the Enneagram to help us find our unique path for transformation as we continue learning and growing. And that's what's super fun about the Enneagram! This insightful tool helps us discover *who we are* and *Whose we are*.

We are not alone on this journey of growth.

God is with us, sustaining us and providing for us. Although we're all uniquely made and no one is alike (it boggles the mind to think about it!), there are commonalities in how we think, feel, and act. The Enneagram shows us nine basic personality Types, each with its own specific patterns of thinking and ways of being: nine *valid* perspectives of the world. Getting to know each of these personality Types increases understanding, compassion, mercy, grace, and forgiveness toward ourselves and others.

Our creative God made us so diverse, yet we all reflect the essence of His character: wise, caring, radiant, creative, knowledgeable, insightful, joyful, protective, and peaceful. As we learn about ourselves and others from the Enneagram, we also learn more about God. Our strengths reflect His attributes.

So how do we begin to find our unique path for growth? By learning about the Enneagram, and by becoming aware of how our heart is doing, which isn't always easy for us. It takes a great deal of time and intentional focus. We start by observing our inner world from a *nonjudgmental* stance. (I don't know how to emphasize this enough!)

Then we can begin to recognize patterns, pause while we are in the present circumstance, and ask ourselves good, clarifying questions about *why* we are thinking, feeling, or behaving in particular ways. We can begin to identify those frustrating patterns we repeat over and over again (the ones we haven't been able to figure out how to stop) and start to think about why we keep doing them.

As I've said before, the Enneagram can act like a rumble strip on a highway, warning you when you're heading off your best path. It lets you know that if you continue in the same direction, drowsy or distracted, you might hurt yourself and others. Alerts about impending danger allow you to course correct, avoid heartache, and experience greater freedom. You will create new patterns of behavior, including a new way of turning to God, when you start to notice the rumble strips in your life.

When you're sensing a rumble strip warning, focus on the acronym AWARE:

- *Awaken*: Notice how you are reacting in your behavior, feelings, thoughts, and body sensations.
- *Welcome*: Be open to what you might learn and observe without condemnation and shame.
- *Ask*: Ask God to help clarify what is happening internally.
- *Receive*: Receive any insight and affirm your true identity as God's beloved child.
- *Enjoy*: Enjoy your new freedom from old self-defeating patterns of living.

Going Deeper

As you look back on your life, when would you have liked a rumble strip to warn you of danger?

_____

_____

_____

_____

_____

_____

In general, what causes you to veer off course and land in a common pitfall (for example, when you're aggressive)?

_____

_____

_____

_____

_____

_____

SHARING WITH OTHERS HOW BEST TO LOVE ME

———————

It is important that you stand
up for yourself and for me.

Demonstrate confidence,
strength, and assertiveness.

I know you see a strong and intense
exterior, but please know that I have
a tender heart that I am protecting.

Acknowledge that I am protective
and providing but don't flatter me.

I can speak bluntly and assertively.
Please don't automatically assume
that this style of relating means
that I am angry or attacking you.

Core Motivations

We'll begin discussing the fundamentals of the Enneagram by looking at our motivations. Your Core Motivations are the driving force behind your thoughts, feelings, and actions. The internal motivations specific to your Type help explain why you do what you do. (This is why it's impossible to discern someone else's Type. We don't know what motivates them to think, feel, and behave in particular ways. It's their Core Motivations, not their actions, that determine their Type.)

These Core Motivations consist of:

- *Core Fear*: what you're always avoiding and trying to prevent from happening
- *Core Desire*: what you're always striving for, believing it will completely fulfill you
- *Core Weakness*: the issue you're always wrestling with, which will remain a struggle until you're in heaven and is a reminder you need God's help on a daily basis
- *Core Longing*: the message your heart longs to hear

The Enneagram, like a nonjudgmental friend, names and addresses these dynamics of your heart. When you use the Enneagram from a faith-centered approach, you can see how Christ's finished work on your behalf has already satisfied your Core Longing and resolved your Core Fear, Core Desire, and Core Weakness. It's a process to learn how to live in that reality.

When we stray from the truth that we are God's beloved children, it's harder to look inside. After all,

Scripture tells us that "the heart is deceitful . . . and desperately sick" (Jeremiah 17:9). When we forget God's unconditional love for us, we respond to our weaknesses and vulnerabilities with shame or contempt, leaving us feeling worse.

When we only focus on obeying externally, we attempt to look good on the outside but never deal with the source of all our struggles on the inside.

However, when we allow ourselves to rest in the truth that Christ took care of everything for us, we can look at our inner world without fear or condemnation. Real transformation begins when we own our shortcomings.

Here are the Core Motivations of a Type 8:

- *Core Fear*: being weak, powerless, harmed, controlled, vulnerable, manipulated, or left at the mercy of injustice
- *Core Desire*: protecting yourself and those in your inner circle
- *Core Weakness*: being lustful/excessive; constantly desiring intensity, control,

and power; willfully pushing yourself and others in order to get what you desire
- *Core Longing*: "You will not be betrayed."

The Enneagram exposes the condition of our heart, and it will tear down any facade we try to hide behind. Since we are God's saved children, we don't have to be afraid of judgment. We can be vulnerable because we know God has taken care of us perfectly through Christ—He has forgiven us and set us free from fear, condemnation, and shame. His presence is a safe place where we can be completely honest about where we are. With this freedom, allow the Enneagram to be a flashlight to your heart's condition. Let it reveal how you are doing at any given moment so you can remain on the best path for your personality Type.

Going Deeper

How challenging is it for you to look at the condition of your heart?

_____

_____

_____

_____

_____

_____

What response do you typically have when you recognize your struggles?

_____

_____

_____

_____

_____

_____

_____

How would you like to respond when the struggles inside you are exposed?

_____

_____

_____

_____

_____

_____

_____

_____

_____

_____

_____

_____

_____

_____

_____

_____

_____

Core Fear

Understanding your Core Fear is the first step in identifying your motivations. Your personality believes it's vital to your well-being that you constantly spend time and energy avoiding this thing you fear. It is the lens through which you see the world, the "reality" you believe. You assume others do, or should, see the world through this lens, and you may become confused and dismayed when they don't.

Your Core Fear as a Type 8 is being weak, powerless, harmed, controlled, vulnerable, manipulated, or left at the mercy of injustice.

You don't want to feel out of control, unsupported, vulnerable, or weak. You don't want to have

your decisions or authority questioned or be surprised by others' unexpected actions.

Even though you fear being weak or betrayed,
here's what is true: God is your protector and
strength.

God sent His Son to rescue you from broken-
ness and to protect you from harm. His triumph
over darkness proves His ability to be your
strength and shield. Believing in Him as your protector allows you to rest instead of striving to be
the most powerful one in charge. He loves you
and has your back.

When your Core Fears get activated, use
them as a rumble strip to alert you. Then pause,
become AWARE, and reorient yourself with what
is true so your heart can rest in His provision and
protection.

MY CORE FEARS

TYPE 8
THE PROTECTIVE CHALLENGER

Being weak, powerless, harmed, controlled, vulnerable, manipulated, and left at the mercy of injustice

Going Deeper

What comes to mind when you think about your Core Fear?

_____

_____

_____

_____

_____

_____

_____

_____

Do any particular words in the Type 8 Core Fear description ring true for you?

_____

_____

_____

_____

_____

_____

_____

_____

_____

_____

What strategies have you used in the past to
protect yourself from your fears?

_____

_____

_____

_____

_____

_____

_____

_____

_____

_____

_____

_____

Core Desire

Understanding your Core Desire is the next step in identifying your motivations. Your Core Desire is what you're always striving for, believing it will ultimately fulfill you.

While your personality Type is running away from your Core Fear, it's also running toward your Core Desire. You believe that once you have this Core Desire met, all of life will be okay and you will feel fully satisfied and content. This longing to experience your Core Desire constantly propels you to focus your efforts on pursuing and obtaining it.

As a Type 8, you desire to protect yourself and those in your inner circle. You seek to have an impact on the world and to stay in control. You want to be self-reliant, assert yourself, prevail over others, and be invincible.

God knows your Core Desire, and He freely gives it to you. He is always with you and watching over you, offering His full protection. He is all-powerful, all-knowing, all-providing, and all-sustaining. He can do anything and handle anything!

When you feel you might be harmed or betrayed, remember you are not left alone. Ask God to care for you and remind you of how He has already protected you throughout your life. Trust that He can give you victory.

Not everyone has the same Core Desire as you. Take time to recognize that others are just as passionate in obtaining their Core Desire as you are in gaining yours. This awareness will help you navigate relationship dynamics, enabling you to offer more empathy, compassion, and grace. Use the Enneagram to know yourself better so you can better communicate with others about what is happening inside your heart. Then be curious

MY CORE DESIRES

TYPE 8
THE PROTECTIVE
CHALLENGER

Protecting yourself and those
in your inner circle

about others, and ask them to reveal to you their desires so you can get to know them on a deeper level.

Going Deeper

As you look back over your life, what aspects of the Type 8 Core Desire have you been chasing?

_____

_____

_____

_____

_____

_____

_____

_____

_____

_____

_____

_____

Describe ways you have attempted to pursue these specific desires.

_____

_____

_____

_____

_____

_____

_____

What would it feel like to trust in the fact that God has already met your Core Desire?

_____

_____

_____

_____

_____

_____

_____

_____

_____

Core Weakness

Deep inside, you struggle with a Core Weakness, which is your Achilles' heel. This one issue repeatedly causes you to stumble in life. At times you might find some relief. But as hard as you try to improve on your own, your struggle in this area continually resurfaces.

God's encouraging words to you are that when you are weak, He is strong. This brings hope that you are not destined to be utterly stuck in your weakness. As you grow closer to God and depend on Him, He will lessen the constraint your Core Weakness has over you and help you move out of your rut.

As a Type 8, your Core Weakness is *lust/excess*.

THE PROTECTIVE CHALLENGER

You constantly desire control, intensity, and power, and willfully push yourself and others to get what you want.

Type 8s are like massive snowplows that can serve a community well after a blizzard. These powerful machines remove obstacles and create clear paths. When you are healthy as a Type 8, you are considerate of others and make sure they are behind your plow, out of harm's way. When you're not as healthy, you become so task-oriented that you charge forward without considering who is in front of you and nick them as you go by. If you allow your lust/excess to go completely unchecked, you can plow right over others.

God is the pure force of life who brought all things into existence. Let Him provide you with a passion for life, a raw and exhilarating intensity that will bring you a sense of vitality and a healthier focus.

When you do, you will be more aware of how you impact others and not only concerned with protecting yourself. By dialing down your intensity from 100 percent to 80 percent, you can honor others' needs while keeping your own pace. You can allow space for others to be themselves instead of aggressively plowing over them, and you can use your amazing gifts of focus, drive, and passion to bless them.

When your see your Core Weakness surfacing, think of it as a rumble strip, alerting you that you can easily veer off course into your common pitfall of constantly asserting your control and power by willfully pushing yourself and others in order to get what you desire. Use this awareness to "recalculate" your inner world so you can get back to your healthiest path.

Going Deeper

What comes to mind as you think about your Core Weakness?

_____

_____

_____

_____

_____

In what ways have you wrestled with lust (the need for intensity, control, and power) throughout your life?

_____

_____

_____

_____

_____

_____

_____

What specific things are you facing now that your Core Weakness impacts?

_____

_____

_____

_____

_____

_____

MY CORE WEAKNESS

TYPE 8
THE PROTECTIVE CHALLENGER

Lust/Excess — constantly desiring intensity, control, and power; willfully pushing yourself on life and others in order to get what you desire

Core Longing

Your Core Longing is the message your heart is always yearning to receive, what you've craved since you were a child. Throughout life, you've been striving to hear this message from your family members, friends, teachers, coaches, and bosses. No matter how much you've tried to get others to communicate this message to you, you've never felt it was delivered to the degree your heart needed it.

As a Type 8, your Core Longing is to hear, "You will not be betrayed."

You have believed that if you could be tough, powerful, and independent enough, then others would communicate this message to you, whether in verbal or nonverbal ways. However, even those who have tried their best to do this for you are unable to satisfy this longing that runs so deep inside you.

Why? Because people *cannot* give you all you need. Only God can. When you're trying to receive this message apart from God, you will always thirst for more. But when you listen to Him and see that He's drawing you to Himself, then you will find fulfillment and freedom.

How does God meet your Core Longing?

1. He is strong and protective.

We all are broken and in desperate need of a rescuer. While you were too weak and unable to heal yourself, God pursued you with His love. He sent His Son to accomplish for you what you could not. He is all-powerful and delights in protecting you.

2. He will neither betray nor forsake you.

You have a true advocate you can trust in God. He took perfect care of you through Jesus, who went through the ultimate betrayal on the cross for you specifically. He conquered death, and nothing can stop Him from protecting you and providing for you. His love is too intensely focused on you, His beloved child. You can truly rest in God's power and strength.

When you feel vulnerable and the need to challenge when it is not needed or beneficial, use the Enneagram as the rumble strip to alert you of what is true; that God will protect you. Allow it to point out how you are believing false messages so you can live a more vulnerable, authentic life with others.

Going Deeper

How have you seen your Core Longing at work in your life?

_____

_____

_____

_____

_____

What did that look like when you were a child?

_____

_____

_____

_____

_____

How does it appear in your life as an adult?

_____

_____

_____

_____

_____

Describe how you feel and what you think when you read that God answers your longing.

_____

_____

_____

_____

_____

_____

TYPE 8
THE PROTECTIVE CHALLENGER

The message my heart always longs to hear.

"You will not be betrayed."

Directional Signals of the Enneagram

Just as a GPS gives directional signals such as "Approaching right turn" or "Proceed to the high-lighted route," the Enneagram guides us in which way to go. But we still need to pay attention to where we're heading and reroute our course when necessary.

The Enneagram provides directions in a couple of ways: (1) by pointing out how aligned with God's truth we are, and (2) by showing us what other Types we are connected to and how we might take on those Types' characteristics in different life situations. We do not *become* the Types we are

HOW TO USE THE ENNEAGRAM
YOUR INTERNAL GPS

It reveals **why** you **think**, **feel**, and **behave** in particular ways, so you can steer your internal life in the best direction for your personality Type.

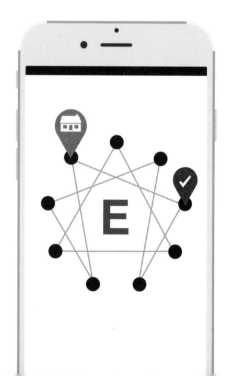

connected to; we remain our Main Type (with its Core Fear, Desire, Weakness, and Longing) as we access the other Types' attributes.

The directional signals of the Enneagram make us aware of which way our heart is heading and where we might end up. Whether it's a good or bad direction depends on various factors—it can change day by day as we take on positive or negative qualities of other Types.

When headed in the wrong direction, the steps to turning around and getting back on track are simply owning our mistakes, turning from them, asking for forgiveness from God and others, and asking God to restore us to the best path.

The directional signals we'll discuss in the following entries are: the Levels of Alignment with God's Truth, the Wings, the Triads, and the Enneagram Paths. Hang in there! I'll guide you through these signals, which will help you discover who you are and Whose you are, and show you the healthiest path for your personality Type.

Type 8 **HOW I TYPICALLY COMMUNICATE**

When I am doing well, I am a generous and loyal friend. I am honest, assertive, and have a confident presence. I stand up for and protect those I care deeply for, the weak, and those at the mercy of injustice.

When I am not doing well, I can be quick to anger, demanding, insensitive, challenging, too assertive and blunt, and refuse to see how I am hurting others.

Levels of Alignment with God's Truth

The first set of directional signals we'll discuss are the Levels of Alignment with God's truth. The inspiration for these levels comes from the apostle Paul, who wrote in Galatians 2:14 that some of the early Christian leaders' conduct was not in step (aligned) with God's truth. To grow in our particular personality Type, we must be in step with God's truth and design for us.

We all move fluidly through the Levels of Alignment from day to day. The level at which we find ourselves at any given moment depends on our heart's condition and how we're navigating through life.

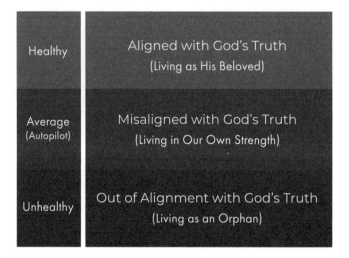

Healthy	Aligned with God's Truth (Living as His Beloved)
Average (Autopilot)	Misaligned with God's Truth (Living in Our Own Strength)
Unhealthy	Out of Alignment with God's Truth (Living as an Orphan)

When we are resting, believing, and trusting in who we are in Christ, we are living as His beloved (healthy and aligned with God's truth). We are no longer using our personality strategies to meet our needs and desires. Instead, we are coming to our God, who we know loves us and will provide for us.

When our heart and mind begin to wander from that truth, we start to believe that we must take some control and live in our own strength, even though He is good and sovereign (average/ autopilot level).

Then there are times when we completely forget that we are His beloved children. In this state of mind, we think we're all alone, that we're orphans who have to handle all of life on our own (unhealthy level).

But no matter where we are on the Levels of Alignment, we are always His cherished children. Christ's life, death, and resurrection accomplished everything required for us to be His. Therefore, no matter what state our heart is in, we can *rejoice* in His work in our lives, *repent* if we need to, and fully *rest* in who we are in Him.

As you can imagine, a group of people with the same personality Type (same Core Fear, Desire, Weakness, and Longing) can look vastly different from each other due to varying alignments with God's truth.

In the readings that follow, we will consider how you as a Type 8 function at the three Levels of Alignment.

Going Deeper

At what Level of Alignment do you think your heart is at the moment?

_____

_____

_____

_____

_____

_____

_____

_____

_____

_____

In what season of life have you thrived the most, not feeling limited by your fears and weaknesses?

_____

_____

_____

_____

What do you think contributed to that growth?

When You Are Aligned

When the condition of your heart is healthy, you align with God's truth that you are fully taken care of by Christ.

As a Type 8 at this level, you use your intensity and power to plow a path for others who cannot plow it for themselves. You have no problem being the one who takes the hits from opposition so that others can move forward in life. You are especially good at advocating for victims of injustice.

You know you are protected and safe in God's care. This enables you to let your tough exterior come down, allowing others to see your tender, gentle, and thoughtful side. You accept that being vulnerable and transparent is a sign of strength, not weakness. You rest in the fact that God will never betray or forsake you.

You become self-restrained, merciful, forbearing, and self-controlled. You are bighearted and courageous, willing to put yourself at risk to bring lasting change for the sake of others.

Going Deeper

When are you at your best and most trusting of God?

_____

_____

_____

_____

_____

_____

_____

_____

What differences do you notice in your thinking and in your life when you're in that state?

_____

_____

_____

_____

_____

_____

_____

What helps you stay in alignment with God's plan for your personality Type?

_____

_____

_____

_____

_____

_____

_____

Write about a time when you've exhibited true generosity, tenderness, compassion, or any other indicators of healthy alignment.

_____

_____

_____

_____

_____

_____

_____

_____

_____

_____

_____

_____

_____

_____

_____

_____

When You Are Misaligned

Even though we know God is good and in control, there are times when our hearts and minds wander away from the truth that God loves us and has fully provided for us in the finished work of Christ on our behalf. In this average or autopilot level of health, we start to believe that we must take some control and live in our own strength.

As a Type 8 at this level, you think it is up to you to protect yourself from being harmed, controlled, or manipulated. Forgetting that God protects you, you use your intensity, strength, and confrontational style to ward off those you believe are trying to hurt you.

You challenge others as a test to see if they are

MY HIDDEN STRUGGLE

TYPE 8

A constant need to look strong
and independent for fear that I'll
be harmed or betrayed if I
expose my tender side

The overall distrust of others
who have the potential to hurt,
mistreat, or control me

The burden of always playing
the role of vigilant protector of
both myself and others

being truthful or trying to take advantage of you, believing that conflict and anger bring out the truth in others. You express your thoughts and opinions bluntly, and if others get hurt by your behavior, you think it is their problem. When confronted, you will not back down. You "say it like it is."

Overall, you operate like a snowplow forcefully pushing everything—including people—out of the way. If you have a task to accomplish and others are in your way, you feel it was their job to have moved. Having little patience for those who are slow to get out of the way, you will not hesitate to finish their task and keep moving forward.

Going Deeper

What aspects of your behavior and life indicate that you are becoming misaligned?

_____

_____

_____

In what ways do you attempt to live in your own strength, not in your identity as a person God loves?

_____

_____

_____

_____

_____

_____

_____

What can you do when you begin to catch yourself in misalignment?

_____

_____

_____

_____

_____

_____

When You Are Out of Alignment Entirely

When we completely forget that our status never changes, and we are still His beloved based on what Christ did for us, we think and believe we're all alone, like an orphan.

Your whole world at this level revolves around protecting yourself from those you believe are a threat. Refusing to trust anyone, you assume everyone has an agenda to hurt or control you. Therefore, you want to beat them to it by controlling them first. If someone has hurt you, you can be very vengeful, ensuring they get what they "deserve."

You may become extremely demanding toward

others, and if your demands are not met, you can become a bully, harming anyone who won't comply. Your intensity, strength, and intimidation can be truly frightening. Most Type 8s, however, do not see their intensity and are surprised by the way others react to it. You do not perceive yourself as dangerous and harmful, but others do.

At this level, you intentionally plow over those you think will harm or control you. Taking matters into your own hands, you do not wait around to see if your suspicions are accurate.

This cycle will continue until you realize that God is a loving, protecting, and caring Father to you. When you begin to believe this truth and depend on Him completely, you will move up the levels of health.

Going Deeper

In what seasons of life have you been most out of alignment with God's truth?

_____

_____

_____

_____

_____

_____

What does this level look like for you (specific behaviors, beliefs, etc.)?

_____

_____

_____

_____

_____

_____

_____

_____

*Who in your life can best support and encourage
you when you're struggling and guide you back to
health?*

_____

_____

_____

_____

_____

_____

_____

_____

_____

_____

_____

_____

_____

_____

_____

_____

_____

_____

The Wings

The next set of directional signals we'll discuss are the Wings, which are the two numbers *directly* next to your Main Type's number on the Enneagram diagram. As I've said, we access the characteristics of the Type on either side of us while remaining our Main Type. So everyone's Enneagram personality is a combination of one Main Type and the two Types adjacent to it.

As a Type 8, your Wings are 7 and 9. You'll often see it written this way: 8w7 or 8w9.

Everyone uses their Wings to varying degrees and differently in different circumstances, but it's common for a person to rely more on one Wing than another.

You can think of the Wings like salt and pepper. Each Wing adds a unique "flavor" to your personality, bringing complexity to your Main Type. Just as a delicious filet mignon doesn't *become* the salt or pepper we season it with, we don't become our Wings. Our Wings influence our Main Type in varying ways, both positively and negatively depending on where we are on the Levels of Alignment. We know that too much salt or pepper can make that filet inedible, but the right balance can enhance our enjoyment of it significantly.

When we align with God's truth, we can access the healthy aspects of our Wings. When we are misaligned or out of alignment with God's truth, we will often draw from the average or unhealthy aspects of our Wings. And like under seasoning or over seasoning our perfectly cooked steaks, it can make a huge difference.

Learning how to use our Wings correctly can dramatically alter our life experiences. Applying "seasoning"—utilizing the healthy attributes of our Wings—can help us change course. As we return to believing and trusting in God, we can express ourselves more fully and be seen for who we really are.

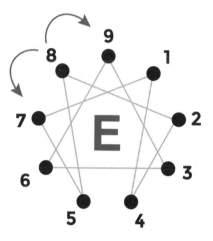

Type 8 with Wing 7 (8w7), The Maverick: These Types blend well together and produce a very confident, aggressive, and assertive subtype. Type 8 wants power, control, and autonomy, and Type 7 wants experiences, possessions, and freedom.

If you're a Maverick, you treat everyone the

same (at home and at work) and insist on others being direct, quick, and assertive. You have a lot of energy, tenacity, perseverance, and confidence. You are much more straightforward, intense, and demanding than the Bear.

When you are struggling, you can focus more on gaining power and control. You may be impatient, demanding, impulsive, and lack compassion for others' feelings.

Type 8 with Wing 9 (8w9), The Bear: These two Types are in conflict with each other. Type 8 is assertive, knows what he or she wants, and moves toward conflicts while Type 9 avoids conflicts and upsetting others.

If you're a Bear, you desire comfort and peace and display more compassion, tenderness, and softness with others. You are less overtly aggressive and hold your power and strength within yourself until it is needed. You are steadier and more patient than the Maverick. You lead others by being calmly supportive and protective.

When you are struggling, your aggressiveness,

Type 8 WINGS

Type 8 with 7 Wing (8w7)
"The Maverick"
They are more extroverted, enterprising, energetic, quick, materialistic, interested in power, and egocentric.

Type 8 with 9 Wing (8w9)
"The Bear"
They are more mild mannered, gentle, receptive, enjoy their comforts, people oriented, and quietly strong.

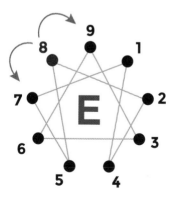

control, and demands come out at work, while your passivity and accommodating qualities remain at home. You can be intimidating to others since they never know when your temper will erupt.

Going Deeper

Which Wing do you use more?

_____

_____

_____

_____

_____

How have you seen this Wing enhance your Main Type?

_____

_____

_____

_____

_____

How does it impact your relationships, work, and everyday life?

_____

_____

_____

_____

_____

_____

_____

_____

_____

How does the other Wing influence your Main Type?

_____

_____

_____

_____

_____

_____

_____

_____

How can you utilize it more to create balance?

_____

_____

_____

_____

_____

_____

_____

_____

_____

_____

_____

_____

_____

_____

_____

_____

_____

_____

_____

_____

The Triads

The next set of directional signals we'll discuss are the Triads. We can group the nine personality Types in many ways, and the most common one is by groupings of three, or Triads. The three Types in each group share common assets and liabilities. For each person one Triad is more dominant (the one with your Main Type) than the other two.

Though we could name several different Triads within the Enneagram, the best known is the Center of Intelligence Triad:

- Feeling Center (Heart Triad): Types 2, 3, and 4
- Thinking Center (Head Triad): Types 5, 6, and 7
- Instinctive Center (Gut Triad): Types 8, 9, and 1

Two commonalities drive the Enneagram Types in each of these three centers: a common emotional imbalance and a common desire.

In the Gut Triad, Types 8, 9, and 1 are imbalanced in their *gut instincts*, having similar assets and liabilities related to those instincts. They all react to their *instinctive struggles with anger*: When Type 8s see an injustice, they respond viscerally in a fast and intense manner. Type 9s, on the other hand, are asleep to their anger because it disrupts their need for peace and harmony. They suppress their anger and are unaware that this is their instinctive struggle. Type 1s repress their anger since they believe anger is bad, but it leaks out through being critical, nitpicky, and judgmental.

Those in the Gut Triad focus on a desire for *justice*. Type 8s do not want the innocent to be harmed, so they will step in and protect. Type 9s do not want others to feel overlooked or unimportant, so they will make space for them to have a voice and be heard. Type 1s do not want unethical injustices to take place, so they will point out what is wrong or inaccurate and fix it.

When you are healthy as a Type 8, you use your incredible intuition to see new possibilities and identify abilities in others that are often overlooked. You also take big and immediate action on behalf of others and for yourself.

When you are struggling, you have trouble relating to the world, because you seek to resist and control your environment. To be unaffected by the external world, you repress your internal fears and

ENNEAGRAM TYPE 8

At Their Best	At Their Worst
Compassionate	Loud
Inspiring	Vengeful
Direct	Excessive
Resilient	Controlling
Loyal	Rebellious
Energetic	Insensitive
Empowering	Domineering
Protective	Self-Centered
Self-Confident	Skeptical

vulnerabilities and will use your aggressive energy (anger) to control and dominate your environment.

As you repress your "softer side" and continue to fear betrayal, you lose your ability to trust and be close to others.

Going Deeper

What stands out to you about being in the Gut Triad and your propensity for intensity and anger?

_____

_____

_____

_____

_____

_____

_____

_____

_____

_____

How attuned are you to your feeling and thinking instincts in comparison to your gut instincts?

_____

_____

_____

_____

_____

_____

_____

In what ways do you wrestle with anger and the need to use strength to protect yourself and others?

_____

_____

_____

_____

_____

_____

Do your efforts to gain power bring the protection you want?

_____

_____

_____

_____

_____

_____

_____

Where do your strengths of passion, focus, drive, and intensity shine the most?

_____

_____

_____

_____

_____

_____

_____

Childhood Message

Before we discuss the last set of directional signals (the Enneagram Paths), we need to understand what the Enneagram calls a Childhood Message.

From birth, everyone has a unique perspective on life, our personality Type's perspective. We all tend toward particular assumptions or concerns, and these develop into a Childhood Message. Our parents, teachers, and authority figures may have directly communicated this message to us, but most of the time, we interpreted what they said or did through the lens of our personality Type to fit this belief.

Sometimes we can see a direct correlation

between our Childhood Message and a childhood event; other times we can't. Somewhere, somehow, we picked up a message that rang true for us because of our personality Type's hardwiring. This false interpretation of our circumstances was and still is painful to us, profoundly impacting us as children and as adults.

Gaining insight into how our personality Type interpreted events and relationships in childhood will help us identify how that interpretation is impacting us today. Believing our Childhood Message causes our personality to reinforce its strategies to protect us from our Core Fear—apart from God's truth. Once we understand the message is hardwired into our thinking, we can experience God's healing truth and live more freely.

What's more, when we know the Childhood Message of others, we can begin to understand why they do what they do and how we can communicate with them more effectively.

As a Type 8, your Childhood Message is: "It is not okay to trust anyone."

The message your heart longed to hear as a child is your Core Longing: "You will not be betrayed."

•   •   •

Type 8 children grew up viewing the world as aggressive and antagonistic, where only those who were strong, tough, and smart survive. They noticed how the weak, innocent, and vulnerable were taken advantage of, hurt, or betrayed, so they decided to put on strong armor to protect themselves from emotional harm.

Whenever their soft and tender hearts were exposed and taken advantage of, they were devastated. Therefore, they rarely removed their armor to allow others to experience their tender side, but when they did, it was an amazing experience.

These children could be confrontational and rebellious. They did not want to be controlled or challenged, so they attempted to control others first. They had intense energy about them that could dominate a whole room. They would command and direct others with confidence.

Type 8s do not trust others easily and worry a lot about betrayal. Many were betrayed in some way growing up, which is where they lost their innocence and decided to put on their protective armor.

Knowing your personality Type's Childhood Message will help you break free from childhood perceptions and reinterpret pieces of your story from a better vantage point. As you explore this, be gracious to yourself and your past. Be sensitive, nonjudgmental, caring, and kind to yourself. And remember, only God can fully redeem your past. He can free you from chains that bind, heal wounds that linger, and restore you to freedom.

Going Deeper

*To what degree do you relate to the Type 8
Childhood Message?*

_____

_____

_____

_____

_____

_____

_____

What stories come to mind when you hear it?

_____

_____

_____

_____

_____

_____

_____

_____

What circumstances in the present have repeated this message from the past?

_____

_____

_____

_____

_____

_____

_____

_____

What advice would you give to your childhood self in light of this message?

_____

_____

_____

_____

_____

_____

_____

_____

Enneagram Paths

The final directional signals we'll discuss are the Enneagram Paths, which the inner lines and arrows in the Enneagram diagram display. The lines and arrows going out from our Main Type point to our Connecting Types. As a Type 8, you connect to Types 5 and 2.

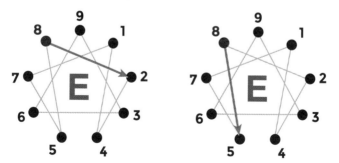

Remember, we can access both positive and negative characteristics of a Type we are connected to. The kind we access depends on whether we are aligned, misaligned, or out of alignment with God's truth.

Here is an overview of the four Enneagram Paths, which we'll discuss further in the following readings:

- *Stress Path*: When we're under stress, we tend to take on some of the misaligned or out-of-alignment characteristics of our Stress Path Type. For Type 8, these are the negative aspects of Type 5.
- *Blind Spot Path*: When we're around those we're most familiar with (mainly family), we display the misaligned characteristics of our Blind Spot Path Type. We typically do not see these characteristics in ourselves easily. For Type 8, these are the negative aspects of Type 2.
- *Growth Path*: When we believe and trust

that God loves us and that all He has is ours in Christ, we begin to move in a healthier direction, accessing the aligned characteristics of our Connecting Type. For Type 8, these are the positive aspects of Type 2.

- *Converging Path*: After making progress on the Growth path, we can reach the most aligned point of our Type, which is where three healthy Types come together. Here we access the healthiest qualities of our Main Type, our Growth Path's Type, and our Stress Path's Type.

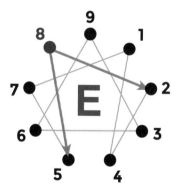

Going Deeper

In what direction is your heart currently heading?

_____

_____

_____

_____

_____

_____

_____

What concerns are you wrestling with?

_____

_____

_____

_____

_____

_____

_____

_____

What growth have you experienced recently?

_____

_____

_____

_____

_____

_____

_____

_____

_____

When you look at the four paths, what path have you been traveling recently? Why?

_____

_____

_____

_____

_____

_____

_____

_____

Stress Path

Under stress, you tend to move in the direction of the arrow below, taking on some of the misaligned characteristics of Type 5. Learning to identify these behavior patterns can serve as a rumble strip warning that you're veering off course. Then you can

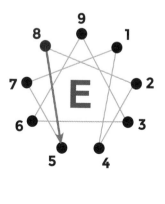

stop, pray for God's help, and move in a healthier direction for your personality.

As a Type 8 moving toward the average or unhealthy Type 5, you may:

- withdraw, become secretive and isolated, and observe from afar.
- detach from emotions and gain more knowledge to be on offense.
- become more cerebral and less physically assertive and action oriented.
- lack trust in people and become cynical and harsh.
- use your intellect to belittle others.

Going Deeper

Describe a stressful time when you took on some of these tendencies.

_____

_____

_____

_____

_____

_____

_____

What was the situation, and why were you triggered to respond this way?

_____

_____

_____

_____

_____

_____

_____

What things in your life cause the most stress
for you?

_____

_____

_____

_____

_____

_____

_____

_____

_____

_____

_____

_____

_____

_____

_____

_____

_____

_____

_____

TYPE 8 UNDER STRESS

When under stress, **Type 8** will start to exhibit some of the average to unhealthy characteristics of **Type 5**.

Becoming secretive and fearful

Becoming less in touch with their feelings and withdraw from others

Fearing that others will turn on them and betray them

Blind Spot Path

When you're around people you're most familiar with—family members or close friends—you express yourself more freely. You show them parts of yourself you don't show anyone else, for better or worse. When you're uninhibited and not at your best, you display the negative qualities of your personality. On this Blind Spot Path, you access the misaligned attributes of your Connecting Type, which is Type 2.

You may be unaware that you're behaving differently with your family members or close friends than you are with other people. Be sure to take note of this path when you're trying to understand yourself and your reactions, because it may surprise you. Working on these negative aspects can improve the relationship dynamics with those you're closest to.

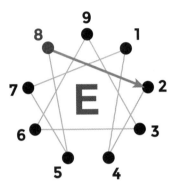

As a Type 8 moving toward the average or unhealthy Type 2, you may:

- need reassurance that those close to you still need you.
- become overly helpful by overstepping relational boundaries and inserting yourself into people's lives without asking.

- desire appreciation for all you do for others.
- feel desperate to hold on to the people in your inner circle, becoming more needy, clingy, and dependent.
- find ways for people to depend on you.

Going Deeper

How do you respond when you feel overwhelmed in the presence of people you feel secure with versus those you're less comfortable with?

Which of the average or unhealthy tendencies do you resonate with the most?

_____

_____

_____

_____

_____

_____

_____

_____

Describe a situation where you reacted in the ways described above.

_____

_____

_____

_____

_____

_____

_____

Growth Path

When you believe and trust that God loves you, and all He has is yours, you begin to relax and let go of your personality's constraints and lies. You draw nearer to Him and move in a direction that aligns you with His truth. You feel safe, secure, and loved.

Feeling more joy, peace, and liberation, you stretch yourself toward healthier attributes, even though it is hard. As you grow in faith and depend solely on Him, God blesses you with real and lasting transformation, shaping you into who He made you to be.

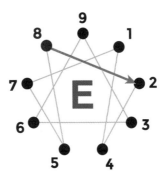

As a Type 8 moving toward the healthy side of Type 2, you can:

- plow a helpful path for others.
- be more thoughtful and caring toward others.
- open up to others and reveal your vulnerable side.
- have more empathy and compassion.
- be more considerate and quicker to serve others.
- put the needs of others above your own.
- show more of your feelings, tender heart, and soft spots.

Going Deeper

When you are growing, what changes about your heart and your typical responses?

_____

_____

_____

_____

_____

_____

Which of these growth attributes would you love to experience more in your life?

_____

_____

_____

_____

_____

_____

What helps to support your growth and flourishing?

_____

_____

_____

_____

_____

_____

_____

How can you incorporate those things into your life more?

_____

_____

_____

_____

_____

_____

_____

_____

TYPE 8 DIRECTION OF **GROWTH**

When moving in the direction of growth, **Type 8** will start to exhibit some of the healthier characteristics of **Type 2**.

Becoming more emotional and generous toward others

Having more empathy and compassion toward others

Opening up to others and revealing their vulnerability

Converging Path

You are your best self on the Converging Path, where three Types come together. Here you access the healthiest qualities of your Main Type, your Growth Path's Type, and your Stress Path's Type. When you live in the fullness of who you really are in Christ, you are freed from the bonds of your personality.

This path of personal transformation can be difficult to reach and maintain. When you first learn about the Converging Path, you may feel it's too hard to travel. But God wants to provide this path for you. Trust Him, follow Him, and ask Him to be with you as you move forward.

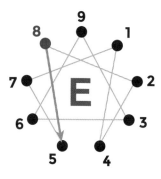

As a Type 8 moving toward the healthy side of Type 5, you may:

- learn humility and your true place in the larger scope of life.
- pause before reacting to your gut instinct, thinking through the best path forward.
- gain more knowledge and insight of your inner world.
- become fascinated with understanding and integrating insightful perspectives.
- observe the gifts and talents of others, creating roles that will let them thrive.

Going Deeper

Can you recall a time when you experienced the freedom and joy of the Converging Path?

_____

_____

_____

_____

_____

What was it like when you accessed the healthiest aspects of your Main Type, Growth Path's Type, and Stress Path's Type?

_____

_____

_____

_____

_____

_____

What would help you move toward your Converging Path more often?

_____

_____

_____

_____

_____

_____

_____

_____

_____

_____

_____

_____

_____

_____

_____

_____

_____

_____

Spiritual Renewal

GOING DEEPER

Grab a journal and write down all the things you try to control and the ways you try to protect yourself. Pray through the list, crossing each item off as you give them to the Lord. Reflect on the truth that Christ's perfect strength and power flow through you, eliminating the need for your protective armor. Write down some ways you can use your passions to benefit others and the greater good.

Moving Toward Your Best Self

The journey of exploring your heart is not an easy one, but it's an exciting one.

God has a unique message for each Type. The message He tells you as a Type 8 is: "You will not be betrayed."

You need someone more powerful than you who can take care of you. God knows precisely what dangers are a threat and is mighty to protect you. You can trust in His strength and ability to deal with every possible concern and hardship in your life.

You believe vulnerability looks like weakness, but the truth is that vulnerability takes a great deal of strength and courage. Jesus was all-powerful yet chose to become vulnerable. He wept and felt deep emotions, such as compassion and sorrow. He washed the feet of His disciples and endured the cross. He could have chosen to destroy everyone and save only Himself, but instead, He took the difficult path that would mean saving and protecting God's cherished children.

Jesus knows how it feels to be betrayed. You can trust Him to care for you. He is the only one who can protect you, and He will never forsake you.

Each Type has a signature Virtue, which you exhibit when you are at your best, and Type 8's Virtue is *innocence/mercy*.

At your best, you are generous, merciful, and forbearing. You act with sensitivity and softness and are careful not to overpower others. Having empathy and compassion, you listen to others' thoughts and feelings without being reactive—or denying your own emotions and weaknesses. You allow others to see your vulnerable side, which deepens your relationships.

You are courageous on behalf of others, using

your strength for their benefit and putting yourself in harm's way for the sake of justice. You have a vision for change and a heart to serve as a tremendous influence for good in the world.

Using the Enneagram from a biblical perspective can empower you to see yourself with astonishing clarity so you can break free from self-condemnation, fear, and shame by experiencing unconditional love, forgiveness, and freedom. In Him, you are whole. And with Him by your side, you can grow stronger and healthier every day.

Now that you know how to use this internal GPS and its navigational signals, start using it every day. Tune in to how your heart is doing. Avoid your common pitfalls by staying alert to your rumble strips. As you learn new awareness and actions, you will move forward on the path that is healthiest for your personality Type and experience the gift of tremendous personal growth.

Going Deeper

What do you notice about yourself when you're at your best?

_____

_____

_____

_____

_____

_____

_____

What would the world be like without the involvement of healthy Type 8s?

_____

_____

_____

_____

_____

_____

_____

Type 8 **VIRTUE**

Innocence/Mercy is your virtue.

This allows you to be present and awake. Your heart is filled with a sweet aliveness and a sense of compassion for the world.

What are some practical ways you can offer your virtue to others today?

Afterword

God's plan to restore the world involves all of us, which is why He made us so vastly different from each other in ways that reflect who He is.

That is why I'm so thrilled you picked up this book and have done the hard, but rewarding, work of looking into your heart. When you align with God's truth, you can support the kingdom, knit people together, and be the best *you* only you can be.

Growth is *not* easy. It requires us to surrender to God, depend on Him, and walk into His calling for us. But when we let go of our control and He takes over, He will satisfy our hearts, filling them with His goodness, and His blessings will flow into our lives and others' lives.

I can attest to God's transformative work having this ripple effect—reaching and positively impacting different parts of our lives and everyone we encounter. As I became more aligned with God's truth (and make no mistake, I'm still in progress!), the changes I was making helped transform my relationships with Jeff, my family, and other people around me. More and more friends, acquaintances, and even strangers were experiencing the transformation that comes from God through the tool of the Enneagram.

I can't wait to look back a year from now, five years from now, or even a decade from now, and hear about the ripple effects *your* transformation has created for hope, wholeness, and freedom. I'm excited about the path of discovery and growth ahead of you! What is God going to do in you with this new understanding of yourself and those around you? What are the things you'll hear Him whisper in your heart that will begin to set you free?

And how will your personal transformation bring positive change to the people in your life?

This is what I hope for you: First, that you will believe and trust in your identity in Christ. In Him, you are forgiven and set free. God delights in having you as His dear child and loves you unconditionally. This reality will radically change everything in you—it is the ultimate transformation from death to life.

Second, I hope that as you discover more about your Enneagram Type, you'll recognize how your personality apart from Christ is running *away* from your Core Fear, running *toward* your Core Desire, *stumbling* over your Core Weakness, and *desperate* to have your Core Longing met. As you become aware of these traits, you can make them the rumble strip alarms that point out what's going on in your heart. Then you can ask the Holy Spirit to help you navigate your inner world and refocus your efforts toward traveling the best path for your personality Type.

Third, I hope that God will reveal to you, both

in knowledge and experience, the transformative work of the Holy Spirit. With Him you can move toward growth, using all the tools of the Enneagram (the Levels of Alignment, the Wings, the Triads, the Enneagram Paths, etc.) to bring out the very best in you, the way God designed you to be. As a result, others will be blessed, God will be glorified, and you will experience the closeness of a Savior who will always meet your every longing and need.

May the love of Christ meet you where you are and pull you closer to God and others. And may you experience the joy of knowing His love for you in a deeper and more meaningful way.

Acknowledgments

My husband: I have to start by thanking my incredible husband, Jeff, who is my biggest cheerleader and supporter. He has helped me use the Enneagram from a biblical perspective and lovingly ensured that I expanded my gifts. Without his encouragement each step of the way, I never would have ventured into this world of writing. Thank you so much, Jeff.

My kids: Nathan and Libby McCord, you are a gift and blessing to me, and an inspiration for the work I do. Thank you for affirming me, being patient with me, and always believing in me. I pray this resource will bless you back as you journey through life.

My family: To my incredible parents, Dr. Bruce and Dana Pfuetze, who have always loved me well and encouraged me to move past difficulties by relying on the Lord. To my dear brother and sister-in-law, Dr. Mark and Mollie Pfuetze, thank you for being a source of support.

My team at Your Enneagram Coach: You enable me to be the best I can be as a leader, and I'm so honored to be a part of our amazing team. Thank you for letting me serve, for showing up every day, and for helping those who want to become more like Christ by using the Enneagram from a biblical perspective. Thank you, Danielle Smith, Traci Lucky, Robert Lewis, Lindsey Castleman, Justin Barbour, and Monica Snyder.

My marketing team, Well Refined Co.: Thank you, Christy Knutson, Jane Butler, JoAnna Brown, and Madison Church.

My agent: Thank you, Bryan Norman, for helping me navigate through all the ins and outs so that this could be the very best work for our readers. Your advice was most beneficial.

My publisher: To Adria Haley and the team at HarperCollins Christian, thank you for allowing me to share my passion for the Enneagram with the world in such a beautiful way through this book collection.

My writing team at StrategicBookCoach.com: Thank you, Danielle Smith, Karen Anderson, and Sharilyn Grayson for helping me create my manuscript.

My friend and advisor: Writing a book is harder than I expected and more rewarding than I could have ever imagined. None of this would have been possible without my most-cherished friend and beloved advisor, Karen Anderson. I am thankful for her heart, her passion, and her help every step of the way. You beautifully take my concepts and make them sing. Thank you!

About the Author

Beth McCord has been using the Enneagram in ministry since 2002 and is a Certified Enneagram Coach. She is the founder and lead content creator of Your Enneagram Coach and cowrote *Becoming Us: Using the Enneagram to Create a Thriving Gospel-Centered Marriage* with her husband, Jeff. Beth has been featured as an Enneagram expert in magazines and podcasts and frequently speaks at live events. She and Jeff have two grown children, Nate and Libby, and live in Franklin, Tennessee, with their blue-eyed Australian Shepherd, Sky.

Continue Your Personal Growth Journey *Just for Type 8!*

Get your Type's in-depth online coaching course that is customized with guide sheets and other helpful insights so you can continue uncovering your personal roadmap to fast-track your growth, overcome obstacles, and live a more fulfilling life with God, others, and yourself.

VISIT YOURENNEAGRAMCOACH.COM/EXPLORING-YOU

The mission of YourEnneagramCoach.com is for people to see themselves with astonishing clarity so they can break free from self-condemnation, fear, and shame by knowing and experiencing unconditional love, forgiveness, and freedom in Christ.